# Spiralìzer:

# Spiralizer Cookbook

## *Healthy And Delicious Spiralizer Recipes*

# Table of Contents

# Introduction

If you are tired of preparing and eating the same pasta dishes, or if you are trying to find healthier alternatives to gluten-rich food, or if you would like to incorporate more vegetables into your (or your family's) diet, then this book is for you.

The spiralizer is a great kitchen tool that can make various shaped *zoodles* (vegetables noodles) in only a few short minutes. You can use it to make savory dishes, delectable snacks, and even refreshing drinks.

This book contains 25 recipes that make the most out of your spiralizer – recipes that are delectable, healthy, and easy-to-follow. To make the most out of your budget, this book recommends freely substituting whatever produce that is most abundant in your area. This way, you get the most out of your money while taking advantage of fruits and vegetables at the peak of their flavors and nutrients. This is also a great way of customizing your recipes to fit your (and your family's) personal taste.

Hopefully, by the time you finish reading this book, you will have great ideas of your own on how to recreate healthier versions of your favorite dishes using your spiralizer.

Also included in this book are a few tips on how to make food preparation and cooking even easier and faster with your machine, and how to properly take care of your spiralizer.

Let's begin the journey.

# Chapter 1: Why Choose the Spiralizer?

Since its introduction into the market, the spiralizer has become an integral part of many kitchens. It is a machine that can slice hardy fruits and vegetables into long noodles. There are those who use these *zoodles* as gluten-free substitutes to the common wheat-based noodles. This is particularly beneficial to people who cannot process gluten (from wheat) for specific health conditions, such as:

- Celiac disease
- Crohn's disease
- Fibromyalgia
- IBS or irritable bowel syndrome
- Lupus
- Rheumatoid arthritis
- Ulcerative colitis
- Wheat allergy
- Wheat intolerance (non-celiac gluten sensitivity)

Others use the spiralizer to follow specific kinds of diet, like:

- Alkaline diet (discourages the consumption of acidic food or those that have low pH levels, like grains, dairy, sugar, meat, etc.)
- Gerson therapy (encourages a low-sodium, low-fat vegetarian diet)
- Gluten-free, casein-free diet (discourages the consumption of all forms of wheat-based food items and drinks, and casein from dairy products)

- Gluten-free / wheat-free diet (discourages the consumption of all forms of wheat-based food, particularly wheat in commercially produced bread and noodles)
- Paleo diet (discourages the consumption of all processed food, including pasta or noodles)
- Raw food diet (encourages the consumption of fresh food sources that does not undergo heating)
- Specific carbohydrate diet (restricts the intake of complex carbohydrates and simple sugars found in grains)
- Veganism (encourages the consumption of more fruits and vegetables and no animal protein,) also similar to
  - Edenic diet (mostly but not exclusively fruits)
  - Juice fasting (mostly vegetable and fruit juices, no solid food)
- Vegetarianism (encourages the consumption of more fruits and vegetables and very little animal protein, if at all,) also similar to
  - Buddhist diet (strict Buddhists follow a vegetarian diet)
  - Fruitarian diet (exclusively fruits)
  - Lacto-vegetarian diet (vegetarian but may eat dairy once in a while)
  - Lacto-ovo diet (vegetarian but may occasionally eat dairy and eggs)

You can of course, use other kitchen tools to make vegetable / fruit noodles (e.g. mandolin, paring knife, vegetable peeler, etc.), but with the spiralizer, you consistently get great looking strands that don't break apart while handling.

This makes the dishes visually appealing, which is always important if you want to your family (kids, in particular) to try something new.

Other benefits of using a spiralizer are:

- It doesn't run on electricity. You don't have to worry about running up a large bill in your monthly utility bills.

- You don't have to miss out on your favorite pasta dishes if you are following a wheat-free diet. *Zoodles* are not only gluten-free, but these cook 100% faster than ordinary pasta. Because most *zoodles* are better served raw or lightly cooked (e.g. blanched,) you consume more fibers and nutrients in the vegetables. This is good for your digestion.

- You can create vibrant looking dishes. Again, because most recipes call for raw or lightly cooked *zoodles*, the vegetables and fruits retain their color and crispness. This is great if you love crunchy greens in fresh salads.

- You consume less calories by simply switching from ordinary pasta to *zoodles*. ½ cup of cooked pasta has 175 to 180 calories. The same amount of *zoodles* has only 40 to 45 calories.

- You can experiment with vegetables and fruits you didn't like using before. Many people love eating vegetables and fruits, but only if someone else prepares these for them! With the spiralizer, you can let your creativity in the kitchen run wild.

- You incorporate more vegetables and fruits in your daily meals. Once you get the hang of using your spiralizer, you will want to use this for almost every meal. By doing so, you inadvertently add more fresh produce into your diet. If you are cooking for kids, this is a great way of gradually introducing them to a healthier eating regimen.

# Chapter 2: A Guide on Spiralizer Blades

Standard spiralizers have 3 blades.

- **Blade A.** This is the widest of all the blades. This is perfect for making long, flat *zoodles*. Vegetables like cucumber and zucchini make the best flat noodles. Because of their wide surface, these tend to absorb more sauce or flavors. Use these *zoodles* in dishes with thick or heavy sauces or gravies. These are also great in hot soups.

  Blade A also makes wafer-thin disks / chips. You can easily make chips from apples, jicama, potatoes, sweet potatoes, etc.

- **Blade B.** This blade has large triangular blades. It makes noodles slightly thicker than regular spaghetti. Vegetables like cucumber, potato and zucchini make the best thick noodles. This is best for meat-heavy pasta dishes, or for cold soups, or for salad dishes with thick dressings.

  You can also make "half-moon" noodles by scoring or making tiny cuts on the surface of the vegetables before pressing these through the blade. Vegetable half-moons can be used for slaws.

- **Blade C.** This blade has tiny triangular blades. It makes noodles slightly thicker than angel hair pasta. Blade C makes the most delicate noodles. You can use almost all kinds of vegetables and fruits with this blade. Thin *zoodles* are perfect for salad dishes with light vinaigrette or pasta dishes with little or no sauces.

You can also make thin noodles to make fritters.

Other spiralizers have an extra cutting implements, like the accordion cutter or the vegetable grater. For the sake of brevity, this book only contains recipes that use the 3 standard blades.

**Fun fact:** The word *zoodles* was coined shortly after the spiralizer was introduced to the public. It was supposed to sell the idea of using zucchini noodles as replacement for wheat-based spaghetti in pasta dishes. Afterwards, *zoodles* became synonymous with any vegetable or fruit-based noodle substitute.

# Chapter 3: Breakfast Food Items

## Recipe #1: Apple Crisps with Peanut Butter Sauce (no cooking required)

Serves 1

*Ingredients:*

For the sauce

➤ 2 Tbsp. milk (or any non-dairy substitute)

➤ 2 Tbsp. organic peanut butter (substitute your choice of chocolate spread or cookie butter if you have peanut allergy)

➤ ¼ tsp. cinnamon powder (if you are not using peanut butter, substitute nutmeg powder)

For the apple crisps

➤ 1 piece, medium apple, whole (substitute: pear)

➤ 2 Tbsp. sweet dry coconut flakes, sweet

➤ 2 Tbsp. raw pecans

➤ handful raw cacao nibs, roughly chopped

➤ drizzle pure maple syrup

➤ drizzle fresh lemon juice

*Directions:*

1. To make the sauce: whisk milk, cinnamon powder and peanut butter until well incorporated. Set aside.

2. <u>To make the apple crisps</u>: brown pecans in a skillet over medium heat until aromatic. Set aside. Roughly chop only when the pecans are cool to the touch.

3. In the same skillet, toast the coconut flakes until golden brown. Set aside to cool completely at room temperature.

4. Using the **Blade A**, slice the apple into small, thin disks. Drizzle a few drops of lemon juice on the cut apples to prevent these from turning brown.

5. Arrange the apple slices on a serving plate. Drizzle these with a little of the peanut butter sauce.

6. Top off with the chopped pecans, toasted coconut flakes, cacao nibs, and maple syrup. Serve immediately.

## Recipe #2: Sweet Apple and Pear Matches

Serves 2

*Ingredients:*

➢ 1 piece, medium apple, whole

➢ 1 piece, medium pear, whole

➢ ¾ cup tapioca flour

➢ ½ cup palm sugar (substitute brown sugar)

➢ 1 Tbsp. cinnamon powder

➢ ½ cup coconut oil

*Directions:*

1. Combine the palm sugar and cinnamon powder in a small bowl. Set aside.

2. Using the **Blade B**, slice the apple and pear into thin sticks. Using a knife, slice the sticks into smaller, more manageable lengths to facilitate faster frying, approximately the length of a match. Immediately dredge the cut fruits into the tapioca flour to prevent these from browning. Just before cooking, shake off the excess flour.

3. Heat the coconut oil in a skillet over medium heat.

4. Carefully slide in the tapioca-coated cut fruits into the hot oil. Fry until golden brown, about 2 minutes or less. Place the cooked "matches" on paper towels to remove the excess grease.

5. Arrange the apple and pear matches on a serving plate and sprinkle with the sugar-cinnamon mixture. Serve while warm.

**Cheat hack:** place a damp tea towel or clean rag underneath your spiralizer before using. This prevents the machine from moving or skidding off the kitchen counter when you process hardier vegetables like carrots and squash. A more expensive option is a silicon mat with a skid-resistant backing. Whatever you choose, always remember: safety first!

## Recipe #3: Cinnamon Apples with Cashew, and Raisins in Oatmeal

Serves 1

*Ingredients:*

➢ 1 piece, medium apple, whole

➢ 1 Tbsp., heaping roasted cashews, lightly salted

➢ 1 Tbsp. raisins

➢ ½ cup steel-cut oats

➢ 1 cup milk (or any non-dairy substitute)

➢ drizzle honey

➢ pinch cinnamon powder

➢ pinch nutmeg

➢ drop vanilla extract

*Directions:*

1. Pour in the steel cut oats and milk in a saucepan set over medium-high. Stir and wait until milk starts to boil. Lower the heat quickly to the lowest setting.

2. Let oats cook for 5 to 10 minutes, stirring often. The oats will thicken after 5 minutes. 3. Remove saucepan from heat. Set aside to cool slightly.

3. Add in the vanilla extract, cinnamon powder, and nutmeg powder to the oats and stir vigorously. This will help aerate the oats.

4. Using **Blade A**, slice the apple into disks. Toss into the oats.

5. Stir in the cashew nuts and raisins.

6. Just before serving, drizzle some honey. Serve while warm.

**Cooking tip:** the best apple varieties to use in the spiralizer are: Cameo, Gala, Fuji, and Granny Smith. These hold up well under the blade, and retain their crunchy texture afterwards. Avoid using baking apples or apples that have too much water content, like: Honey Crisp, McIntosh, and Red Delicious.

## Recipe #4: Plantain Pancake

Serves 2

*Ingredients:*

➤ 2 pieces, medium almost ripe plantains, choose the ones that are slightly firm to the touch and not mushy

➤ 2 Tbsp., heaping all-purpose flour

➤ 1 piece, medium egg, lightly beaten

➤ 1 tsp. white sugar

➤ ¼ tsp. baking powder

➤ ¼ cup milk or water

➤ dash nutmeg

➤ dash powdered sugar

➤ drop vanilla extract

➤ canola oil, just enough to shallow fry the pancakes

*Directions:*

1. Except for the plantains, powdered sugar and cooking oil, pour the rest of the ingredients into a bowl. Mix well to remove visible lumps. Set aside.

2. Using **Blade A**, chop the plantains into small, thin disks. Drop these into the batter.

3. Place a skillet over medium heat. Pour in a small amount of oil and swirl it around so that the cooking surface is lightly coated.

4. Carefully ladle in ½ cup of the plantain batter into the hot oil. Let the pancake cook for 1 to 3 minutes on the first side, or

until the edges are set and bubbles form in the middle. Flip the pancake and cook the other side for another minute. Do not press down. Transfer the cooked pancake into a serving plate.

5. Repeat step #4 until all the batter is cooked.

6. Stack the pancakes and sprinkle with a little powdered sugar. Serve while warm.

**Cooking tip:** always cut your *zoodles*. Although long noodles are fun to make, these are difficult to cook and eat. Cutting your *zoodles* is also a great way of controlling portions.

**Recipe #5: Curly Plantain Fries**

Serves 2

*Ingredients:*

- ➤ 2 pieces, medium unripe plantains (substitute sweet potatoes or squash)
- ➤ 1 Tbsp., heaping all-purpose flour
- ➤ 1 tsp. corn meal
- ➤ 1 piece, medium egg, lightly beaten
- ➤ dash sea salt or kosher salt
- ➤ canola oil, just enough to deep fry the plantains

*Directions:*

1. Combine all-purpose flour and corn meal in a bowl. Set aside.
2. Using **Blade B**, slice the plantains into long, thick noodles. Drop these into the egg. Gently submerge for even coating.
3. Dredge the fries into the flour-cornmeal mix.
4. Place a skillet over medium heat. Pour in the oil.
5. Place a few pieces of flour-coated plantains into the hot oil. Cook for 2 to 5 minutes or until golden. Cooking time would depend on how long your curly fries are.
6. Place the fries on paper towels to remove the excess grease.
7. Repeat steps #5 and #6 until all the plantains are cooked.
8. Just before serving, sprinkle the fritters with a little sea salt. Cool slightly before serving.

**Cooking tip:** the best plantains to use for *zoodles,* fries, and fritters are semi-unripe ones. These should still be green colored, but the flesh should yield slightly when pressed. The skin should come right off. For crisps, use unripe ones. These should be dark green in color, and you have to use a knife to peel off the skin. These should be sliced as thinly as possible. Unripe plantain crisps should be cooked in a lot of oil.

# Chapter 4: Quick Salad and Lunch Ideas

### Recipe #6: Beetroot, Carrot and Radish Salad on Watercress with Walnut Dressing

Serves 2

*Ingredients:*

<u>For the dressing</u>
- ➤ 4 Tbsp. extra virgin olive oil
- ➤ 2 Tbsp. freshly squeezed lemon juice
- ➤ 1 piece, small garlic clove, grated
- ➤ 1 tsp. Dijon mustard (for a spicier mix, substitute English mustard)
- ➤ ½ tsp. honey
- ➤ salt, to taste
- ➤ white pepper, to taste
- ➤ ¼ cup walnuts

<u>For the salad</u>
- ➤ 1 piece, large raw sugar beets
- ➤ 1 piece, small carrot
- ➤ 1 piece, large radish
- ➤ 4 slices halloumi (or any grilling cheese like: *kefalotyri, queso panela,* or provolone)

> ➤ 2 handfuls, generous watercress, rinsed, drained

*Directions:*

1. <u>For the dressing</u>: in a dry skillet, toast the walnuts until slightly brown and aromatic. Cool slightly before chopping. Set aside.

2. In a mason jar (or any container with a tight-fitting lid,) add in the remaining ingredients. Seal the jar and shake well to combine. Set aside.

3. <u>For the salad</u>: place two generous handfuls of watercress on a serving plate. Place in the fridge to chill.

4. Peel the beetroot, radish, and carrot. Using **Blade C**, turn the vegetables into thin *zoodles*. Place in the fridge to chill.

5. In a non-stick pan, gently grill the halloumi slices until brown on both sides, about 3 to 4 minutes. Allow the halloumi to cool before slicing into thin strips.

6. <u>To assemble</u>: pour in 2 tablespoons of the dressing into the bowl of vegetables. Add in the chopped walnuts and sliced halloumi. Toss well to combine. Place salad on the chilled plate of watercress. Add more dressing, if desired. Serve immediately.

**Salad tip:** always dress your salad greens at the last minute, then serve immediately. This prevents vegetables and fruits from turning limp and soggy. If you are not sure if the salad will be eaten right away, you can toss the salad at the table, and serve the dressing on the side.

Another tip to preserve the crunchiness of leafy greens is to spin-dry (use a salad spinner) the vegetables after rinsing. This quickly removes most of the moisture without damaging the fragile leaves.

## Recipe #7: Chilled Cucumber Noodles with Tomato-Basil Vinaigrette

Serves 2

*Ingredients:*

### For the dressing

➤ 6 to 12 pieces, large fresh basil leaves, roughly chopped

➤ 1 can chopped tomatoes, lightly drained

➤ 1 clove, large garlic, grated

➤ 2 Tbsp. fresh lemon juice

➤ 2 Tbsp. extra virgin olive oil

➤ ¼ tsp. lemon zest

➤ salt, to taste

➤ white pepper, to taste

### For the salad

2 pieces, large cucumbers, ends removed

1 cup ripe cherry tomatoes, quartered

1 cup baby spinach or arugula, rinsed, drained

4 slices, thin feta cheese, roughly torn

6 pieces quail eggs, hard-boiled, shelled, halved

*Directions:*

1. <u>For dressing</u>: combine all the ingredients in a small bowl. Adjust seasoning according to taste. Use salt sparingly because the feta cheese in the salad will be slightly salty. Set aside in the fridge to chill for at least 15 minutes.

2. <u>For the salad</u>: Using **Blade B**, turn both cucumbers into thick *zoodles*. Toss these, along with the rest of the salad ingredients (except for the quail eggs) into a large bowl.

3. <u>To assemble</u>: lightly drizzle the salad with a tablespoon of the chilled dressing. Toss well to combine. Plate the salad and add more dressing, if desired.

4. Dot the salad with the quail eggs. Serve immediately.

# Recipe #8: Spicy Green and Yellow Mango Salad

Serves 2

*Ingredients:*

## For the dressing

- 2 Tbsp. extra virgin olive oil
- 1 Tbsp. fresh lime juice
- 1 Tbsp. apple cider juice, or apple vinegar
- 1 Tbsp. honey
- 1 tsp. Dijon mustard
- ¼ tsp. fresh lime zest
- salt, to taste
- white pepper, to taste

## For the salad

- 1 cheek, medium green mango, peeled
- 1 cheek, medium ripe mango, peeled, julienned
- 1 piece, medium carrot, peeled
- 1 piece, medium zucchini, unpeeled
- 1 piece, large fresh jalapeno, halved, julienned
- ¼ piece, small unripe or green papaya, peeled, deseeded
- handful fresh cilantro, roughly chopped, for garnish

*Directions:*

1. <u>To make the dressing</u>: in a mason jar, (or any container with a tight-fitting lid,) add all the ingredients of the dressing. Seal and shake well to combine. Set aside.

2. <u>To make the salad</u>: using **Blade C**, turn the green mango cheek, unripe papaya, carrot, and zucchini into thin *zoodles*.

3. Toss these, along with the rest of the salad ingredients (except for the cilantro) into a large bowl.

4. <u>To assemble</u>: drizzle half of the dressing into salad. Toss well to combine. Plate the salad and garnish with cilantro. Drizzle more dressing, if desired. Serve as is, or as a side to a meat-based dish. Serve immediately.

## Recipe #9: Hot Sausage Salad with Cucumber and Zucchini

Serves 3 to 4

*Ingredients:*

- ½ link smoked / dried Hungarian sausage, sliced diagonally into ½ inch thick disks
- ½ link smoked / dried Hungarian sausage, sliced diagonally into ½ inch thick disks
- ½ link smoked / dried Hungarian sausage, sliced diagonally into ½ inch thick disks
- ½ link regular hotdog or frankfurter, sliced diagonally into ½ inch thick disks
- 2 Tbsp. white wine vinegar
- 1 Tbsp. black or red peppercorns, freshly cracked
- 1 tsp. olive oil
- 1 tsp. sugar
- 1 piece, large white onion, thinly sliced
- 1 piece, large bird's eye chili, minced
- 1 piece, small red bell pepper, julienned
- 1 piece, medium zucchini, chilled for 20 minutes
- 1 piece, medium cucumber, chilled for 20 minutes
- ½ piece, medium lemon, juice only
- pinch sea salt
- 4 to 6 stalks parsley, roughly chopped, for garnish (optional)

*Directions:*

1. <u>To make the sausage salad</u>: pour oil into a large frying pan set over medium heat. 2. 2. Carefully place all the sausages into the hot oil. Cook until most of the slices curl at the edges, stirring often. Remove pan from heat.

2. In a small bowl, dissolve the sugar in the white wine vinegar. Stir in the black peppercorns. Pour mixture into the pan.

3. Add in the onion slices, chili and red bell pepper. Toss salad in the pan to combine.

4. Using **Blade A**, slice both the cucumber and zucchini into long, flat *zoodles*. Slice into 4-inch long strands. Place into a bowl and toss with the lemon juice and a pinch of salt. Place these on a large serving platter.

5. Pour the still warm sausage salad on top of the *zoodles*. Garnish with parsley, if using. Serve immediately.

### Recipe #10: Cucumber, Jicama, and Zucchini Salad with Egg and Tuna Dressing

Serves 3 to 4

*Ingredients:*

For the dressing

- ➤ 2 pieces, large soft-boiled eggs, shelled, roughly chopped
- ➤ 1 pieces, medium celery stalks, minced
- ➤ 1 can, 5 oz. / 124 g. tuna chunks in water or brine, drained
- ➤ ½ cup plain Greek yogurt
- ➤ 2 Tbsp. mayonnaise
- ➤ ¼ tsp. garlic powder
- ➤ ¼ tsp. sea salt
- ➤ dash black pepper

For the salad

- ➤ 1 piece, medium zucchini, unpeeled, chill before using
- ➤ 1 piece, small cucumber, unpeeled, chill before using
- ➤ ¼ piece, medium jicama, peeled, chill before using

*Directions:*

1. To make the dressing: pour all the ingredients into a bowl. Using a rubber spatula, gently fold everything until tuna flakes are well-coated. Set aside to chill in the fridge for at least 20 minutes.

2. <u>To make the salad</u>: Using **Blade A**, turn your jicama into flat noodles. Cut into 4 inch long strips.

3. Using **Blade B**, turn your cucumber into thick noodles. Cut into 4 inch long strips.

4. Using **Blade C**, turn your zucchini into thin noodles. Cut into 4 inch long strips.

5. <u>To assemble</u>: combine all the *zoodles* in a large salad bowl. Pour half of the dressing into the vegetables. Gently toss to combine.

6. Plate one portion of salad. Add more dressing, if desired. Serve immediately.

# Chapter 5: Dinner Ideas and Pasta Dishes

### Recipe #11: Cucumber Pasta in White Sauce

Serves 2

*Ingredients:*

1 piece, large cucumber

<u>For the béchamel</u>

➤ 1 Tbsp. unsalted butter

➤ 1 Tbsp. olive oil

➤ 1 Tbsp., heaping all-purpose flour

➤ ½ cup *Pecorino Romano*, grated, add more later, for garnish

➤ 1½ cup chicken or beef stock, divided (for a creamier sauce, substitute ¾ cup of chicken stock + ¾ cup milk)

➤ dash black pepper

➤ dash nutmeg

*Directions:*

1. Using **Blade B,** turn the cucumber into thick *zoodles.* Slice into 6-inch long strands. Set aside.

2. <u>To make the béchamel</u>: in a saucepan, pour in the olive oil and butter. Set the pan over medium heat, but turn it down to the lowest setting once the butter melts.

3. Whisk in the flour until the flour clumps together. Pour in half of the chicken stock while stirring constantly.

4. Stir in the grated cheese, black pepper and nutmeg.

5. After a few minutes, the sauce will thicken. If the sauce is too thick, gradually add in the remaining stock. The sauce is done when it coats the back of the ladle. Remove pan from the heat. Let the sauce cool for at least 5 minutes before adding in the *zoodles*. Toss well to combine.

6. 6..Plate into individual portions. Top off with more cheese, if desired. Serve immediately.

## Recipe #12: Sweet Potato Pasta with Savory Asparagus Sauce

Serves 3 to 4

*Ingredients:*

➢ 1 piece, small sweet potato

➢ 6 spears, large asparagus, tough ends snapped off

➢ 6 stalks parsley, roughly chopped, for garnish

➢ ½ cup *Pecorino Romano*, grated, add more later for garnish


For the sauce

➢ 2 links, medium fresh Italian sausages, casings removed, crumbled

➢ 2 Tbsp. olive oil, divided

➢ 1 clove, large garlic, minced

➢ ½ cup chicken or beef stock

➢ ¼ tsp. red pepper flakes

➢ black pepper, to taste

➢ salt, to taste


*Directions:*

1. Using **Blade B**, turn the sweet potato into thick *zoodles*. Slice into 6-inch long strands. Set aside.

2. Using a vegetable peeler, shave the asparagus into ribbons. Set aside.

3. <u>To make the sauce</u>: pour oil in a saucepan set over medium heat.

4. Stir fry the sausage meat 5 to 7 minutes until golden brown, while breaking up larger clumps.

5. Toss in the sweet potato *zoodles,* garlic, and red pepper flakes. Stir gently.

6. Pour in the chicken broth and bring to a boil. Turn down the heat to a simmer. Cook the sweet potato noodles 3 to 5 minutes.

7. Turn the heat off before tossing in the asparagus. Sprinkle in the cheese, salt and pepper.

8. <u>To assemble</u>: place pasta on to a plate. Garnish with parsley, if using. Serve.

## Recipe #13: Butternut Squash with Chicken Tikka Masala

Serves 2 to 3

*Ingredients:*

- ➢ 1 piece, small butternut squash, peeled, halved, deseeded
- ➢ ½ tsp. garlic powder
- ➢ salt, to taste
- ➢ white pepper, to taste

For the sauce

- ➢ 2½ Tbsp. olive oil, divided
- ➢ 1 pound chicken thigh fillets, diced (substitute pork tenderloin or grouper fillets,) seasoned with a little...
- ➢ salt
- ➢ 2 pieces, medium onions, minced
- ➢ 2 cloves, large garlic, minced
- ➢ 1½ Tbsp. *garam masala*
- ➢ 1 Tbsp. ginger, grated
- ➢ 1 Tbsp. fresh lemon juice
- ➢ 2 tsp. cumin powder
- ➢ 1½ tsp. coriander powder
- ➢ ½ tsp. turmeric powder
- ➢ ¼ tsp. cayenne pepper powder
- ➢ 1½ cups canned tomato puree

> ¼ cup Greek yogurt, plain

> 12 stalks fresh cilantro, roughly chopped, for garnish

*Directions:*

1. <u>To make the noodles</u>: using **Blade B**, turn the squash halves into thick *zoodles*. Slice into 6-inch long strands. Place these on a baking sheet lined with parchment paper. Drizzle with ½ tablespoon of olive oil. Season well with garlic powder, salt and pepper.

2. Bake the *zoodles* in a 400°F or 205°C preheated oven for 8 to 10 minutes, or until the squash is fork tender. Remove the baking sheet immediately out of the oven, and let cool to room temperature.

3. <u>To make the chicken masala sauce</u>: pour 1 tablespoon of olive oil into a large saucepan set over medium heat.

4. Add in the diced chicken, a handful at a time. Brown the chicken pieces on all sides then transfer to a bowl. Continue until all chicken pieces are seared. Set aside.

5. In the same saucepan, pour in the remaining oil. Stir fry the onion, garlic and ginger until onion turns limp and translucent.

6. Add in the spice mix: *garam masala,* cayenne pepper, coriander, cumin, and turmeric powder.

7. Stir in the tomato puree. Put the lid on and let the stew come to a boil.

8. Remove lid. Add in the chicken, then turn down the heat to simmer. Cook the chicken until tender, about 15 to 20 minutes.

9. Remove pan from heat. Stir in the lemon juice and yogurt.

10. <u>To assemble</u>: plate a portion of the *zoodles*. Pour a ladleful of chicken tikka masala on top. Garnish with cilantro. Serve while warm.

**Cooking tip:** Always align your vegetables as straight as possible within the brackets of the spiralizer. This will ensure that you get uniform-sized noodles. But making odd shapes in your spiralizer is fun to do too! Odd shapes are great for light salads, soups, and stews.

# Recipe #14: Beet Gnocchi with Feta and Pecans

Serves 2

*Ingredients:*

For the salad

➢ 2 pieces, large beets, choose firm ones, peeled
➢ ¼ cup feta cheese, crumbled
➢ ¼ cup pecans, lightly roasted, lightly salted

For the dressing

➢ 4 Tbsp. olive oil, divided
➢ 4 Tbsp. light honey
➢ 4 Tbsp. red wine vinegar
➢ 1 piece, large shallots, minced
➢ salt, to taste
➢ black pepper, to taste

*Directions:*

1. To make the dressing: in a mason jar (or any container with a tight-fitting lid,) add in all the ingredients. Seal the jar. Shake well to combine. Set aside.

2. To make the salad: using **Blade A,** turn the beets into small disks. Place the disks on a baking sheet lined with parchment paper. Drizzle with ½ tablespoon of olive oil. Season with a little salt and pepper.

3. Bake the beets in a 400°F or 205°C preheated oven for 7 to 10 minutes, or until the vegetable is slightly mushy but still retains its shape. Remove the baking sheet immediately out of the oven, and let cool to room temperature.

4. To assemble: place the cooked beets in a large salad bowl. Add in half of the pecans, half of the crumbled feta cheese, and half of the dressing. Toss well to combine. Do not be alarmed if the beet breaks into smaller pieces.

5. Spoon a portion into a plate. Top off with more pecans, feta cheese and dressing, if desired. Serve immediately.

# Recipe #15: Turnip Risotto with Broccoli Pesto

Serves 2 to 3

*Ingredients:*

## For the turnip risotto

2 pieces, large turnips, peeled

## For the broccoli pesto

- ➤ 1 head, small broccoli, cut into small florets, steamed for 5 minutes or until fork tender, shocked in an ice bath, then drained well
- ➤ 1½ cups, packed fresh basil leaves
- ➤ 1 clove, large garlic, minced
- ➤ 2 Tbsp. pine nuts, lightly roasted, lightly salted
- ➤ 1 Tbsp. olive oil
- ➤ 1 Tbsp. Parmesan cheese, grated, add more later for garnish
- ➤ ¼ tsp. olive oil
- ➤ ½ tsp. sea salt
- ➤ ¼ tsp. black pepper
- ➤ 1 pinch red pepper flakes
- ➤ salt, to taste
- ➤ black pepper, to taste

<u>For garnish</u>

3 pieces, large eggs, lightly poached, lightly salted

*Directions:*

1. <u>To make the turnip risotto</u>: using **Blade C**, turn the turnip into thin *zoodles*. Place the noodles into a food processor and pulse once or twice. Do not over process or your risotto will turn into mush. If you do not have a food processor, roughly chop the *zoodles* to make these smaller, or about the size of long-grained rice. Place the risotto on paper towels to remove excess moisture.

2. <u>To make the broccoli pesto</u>: except for the cooked broccoli, place all the ingredients into the food processor. Process until smooth.

Season lightly with salt and pepper.

Add the broccoli and pulse quickly once or twice. Some of the broccoli florets should remain bite-sized.

3. <u>To assemble</u>: toss the turnip risotto and broccoli pesto into a large salad bowl. Ladle a portion on a plate. Sprinkle more cheese on top, if desired.

Top off each portion with a poached egg. Serve immediately.


**Cooking tip:** always wear gloves and an apron when preparing beets. It takes days before the crimson color wears off on skin. Beet juice on cloth usually don't fade, even after using powerful stain removal agents. After slicing, immediately soak the spiralizer and the blades in soapy water to prevent the juice from permanently ruining the color of your machine.

# Easy Soups and Stews

### Recipe #16: Hot Egg Drop Soup

Serves 3 to 4

*Ingredients:*

- 1 piece, large egg, lightly beaten
- 1 piece, small zucchini
- 2 cups vegetable stock / broth
- ½ cup water
- 3 Tbsp. *Kombu* or *nori* flakes
- 1 Tbsp. ginger, grated
- 1 Tbsp. light soy sauce
- ¾ Tbsp. extra virgin olive oil
- 2 tsp. rice vinegar
- ¼ tsp. red pepper flakes
- black pepper, to taste
- ½ cup scallions, roughly chopped, for garnish (optional)

*Directions:*

1. Using **Blade C**, turn the zucchini into thin *zoodles*. Slice into 4-inch long strands. Set aside.

2. To make the soup: pour oil and ginger in a large saucepan set over high heat. Stir fry the ginger until aromatic (about a minute) before adding in the red pepper flakes, soy sauce, vegetable broth, vinegar, and water. Let the soup come to a boil.

3. Turn down the heat to simmer. Add the seaweed flakes.

4. Gently pour in the egg while stirring often. The egg should cook in less than 30 seconds.

5. Turn off the heat. Season the soup with black pepper. Let the soup cool slightly before serving.

6. <u>To assemble</u>: place a few strands of *zoodles* in a soup bowl. Ladle out a good portion of egg drop soup in the bowl. Garnish with scallions, if using. Serve while warm.

# Recipe #17: Italian Meatball Stew with *Zoodles* (Slow Cooker Recipe)

Serves 4

*Ingredients:*

## For the stew

- ➤ 1 piece, large zucchini
- ➤ 4 cups beef or chicken stock
- ➤ 2 pieces, large celery stalks, roughly chopped
- ➤ 2 pieces, large tomatoes, deseeded, quartered
- ➤ 1 piece, large onion, quartered
- ➤ 1 piece, small apple, cored, quartered
- ➤ 1 piece, small carrot, roughly chopped
- ➤ 1 piece, small potato, roughly chopped
- ➤ 1 piece, small sweet potato, roughly chopped

## For the meatballs

- ➤ 1 Tbsp. olive oil
- ➤ 1½ pound ground beef, 75% to 85% lean
- ➤ 1 piece, large egg, whole
- ➤ 6 cloves, large garlic, minced
- ➤ 1 piece, large onion, minced
- ➤ ½ cup steel rolled oats
- ➤ ½ cup Parmesan cheese, grated

- 1 Tbsp. fennel fronds, minced
- 1½ tsp. garlic salt
- 1½ tsp. sea salt
- 1½ tsp. onion powder
- 1 tsp. oregano powder
- 1 tsp. Italian seasoning or *Herbes De Provence*
- ½ tsp. black pepper

*Directions:*

1. <u>To make the meatballs</u>: except for the olive oil, combine all the ingredients in a large mixing bowl. Mix only until the oats are well incorporated. Do not overwork the meat.

2. Line a baking sheet with parchment paper. Roll the beef mix into 1½ inch thick meatballs. Let the meat rest on the baking sheet for at least 30 minutes before cooking. Chill in the fridge if possible.

3. When you are ready to cook, pour the olive oil in a skillet set over medium heat.

4. Shallow fry the meatballs in batches, flipping often until most of the sides have browned. Place the partially cooked meatballs into a separate bowl. Repeat this step until all the meatballs are seared.

5. <u>To make the stew</u>: set the slow cooker on the highest setting. Place all the vegetables and fruits into the slow cooker pot (apple, carrot, celery, onion, potato, sweet potato and tomatoes.)

6. Pour in the beef stock.

7. Gently drop each meatball into the beef stock. Put the lid on.

8. Turn down the slow cooker to its lowest setting and let the stew cook for another 3 hours.

9. Partially remove the lid. Let the stew cool down for at least 10 minutes.

10. To serve: prepare the zucchini using **Blade A**. Make 6 inch-long flat noodles. Place a handful of noodles in a deep bowl.

11. Ladle beef stew on top of the *zoodles*. Serve while warm.

**Cooking tip:** use medium to large fruits and vegetables in your spiralizer for easier and faster processing. One large zucchini can yield about two cups of *zoodles* in one processing. Three small zucchini will also yield about 2 cups, but you need to exert three times the effort.

## Recipe #18: Stir Fry Beef Steak and Broccoli

Serves 2

*Ingredients:*

### For the beef

- ➤ 2 pieces, 5 oz. each, beef sirloin steaks or rib eye steaks, fat trimmed
- ➤ ¼ cup hoisin sauce
- ➤ ¼ cup fresh squeezed lemon juice
- ➤ 2 Tbsp. light soy sauce
- ➤ pinch red pepper flakes
- ➤ dash white pepper flakes
- ➤ 1 Tbsp. olive oil

### For the stir fry

- ➤ 2 pieces, large broccoli with stems
- ➤ 1 piece, small onion, finely sliced
- ➤ 1 piece, thumb-sized fresh ginger, grated
- ➤ 1 clove, large garlic, minced
- ➤ 1 tsp. sesame oil
- ➤ ½ tsp. corn flour

*Directions:*

1. <u>To marinate the beef</u>: place steaks in a freezer-safe bag. Pour in hoisin sauce, lemon juice, red pepper flakes, white pepper, and soy sauce. Seal the bag, removing as much air as possible. Massage the marinade into the meat before storing the bag into the fridge (not the freezer) for at least 30 minutes. (Overnight is better.)

2. When you are ready to cook, preheat the oven to 400°F or 205°C.

3. On the stovetop, pour oil into an oven-safe skillet set over medium heat.

4. Remove steaks from the bag. Gently shake off marinade, and reserve the rest for the stir-fry.

5. Wait for the oil to become slightly smoky before placing in the steaks.

6. Sear one side of the steak until lightly browned, about 3 to 5 minutes. Flip, and cook the other side for another 3 minutes.

7. Cover the skillet with aluminum foil, then place the entire skillet in the preheated oven. Bake the steaks for 20 minutes.

8. Immediately remove the skillet from the oven. Without removing the aluminum foil, let the steaks rest for the next 10 minutes.

9. Take the steaks out of the pan. (Use this same skillet for the stir-fry.)

10. Slice the steaks across the grain as thinly as possible. Set aside.

11. <u>To make the stir-fry</u>: slice the broccoli tops into bite-sized florets, reserving the stem. 12. Chop off the tough lower ends of the broccoli. Peel the stems. Using **Blade B**, turn the broccoli stem into *zoodles*.

12. Pour marinade in a bowl and dissolve the corn flour in it.

13. Set the same skillet over medium heat. Toss in the aromatics: onion, ginger and garlic. Stir-fry until onion is limp and transparent.

14. Toss in the broccoli florets and stir-fry for 2 minutes.

15. Add in the sliced steaks, *zoodles,* and the marinade-corn flour mix. Cook for a further 2 minutes until you have thick sauce. Turn off the heat.

16. Just before serving, drizzle in the sesame oil. Ladle one portion on a plate and serve while warm.

**Cooking tip:** when marinating meat, you should do so for the longest time possible. This will not only deepen its flavor, but it will also tenderize the meat. If you are in a hurry, you can "cheat" by first pounding the fillets with a meat mallet, then marinating it.

## Recipe #19: Spinach and Zucchini Lasagna with Cheesy Mushroom Sauce

Serves 2

*Ingredients:*

- ➢ 4 pieces, large fresh portabella mushrooms, stemmed, thickly sliced
- ➢ 2 pieces, large zucchini
- ➢ 1 piece, large egg, lightly beaten
- ➢ 1 piece, large onion, minced
- ➢ 1 clove, large garlic, minced
- ➢ 3 cups spaghetti sauce, with…
- ➢ 1 tsp. sugar
- ➢ 2 cups, packed frozen spinach, thawed, drained, minced
- ➢ 3 cups ricotta or any fresh, soft cheese
- ➢ 3 cups buffalo mozzarella, roughly torn
- ➢ 1¾ cups Romano or Parmesan cheese, freshly grated, divided
- ➢ 2 Tbsp. olive oil, divided
- ➢ 1 tsp. sea salt
- ➢ 1 tsp. oregano powder
- ➢ 1 tsp. basil powder
- ➢ ½ tsp. black pepper

*Directions:*

1. Preheat the oven to 350°F or 175°C.

2. Using **Blade A**, turn your zucchini into long, thin *zoodles*. Slice these approximately to the length of your baking dish. Set aside.

3. Microwave the spaghetti sauce and sugar together at the highest setting for 10 seconds. Mix well. Set aside.

4. Set a skillet over medium heat. Pour in one tablespoon of olive oil. Sear a handful of the sliced mushrooms. Flip. Sear the other side. Transfer mushrooms to a plate. Continue cooking until all the mushrooms are seared.

5. Pour in the remaining oil. Stir fry the onion and garlic together, until onion is limp and transparent, about 2 to 3 minutes. Add in the spinach and seared mushrooms. Cook while stirring often (but gently,) until the leaves are dark and limp, about 5 minutes. Remove pan from heat. Let this cool completely at room temperature.

6. In a large bowl, combine the cooked spinach, mushrooms, ricotta cheese, ¾ Romano cheese, egg, oregano, basil and pepper. Fold gently.

7. To assemble the lasagna: ladle ¼ portion of the spinach-mushroom mix at the bottom of the baking dish. (There should be enough so that this becomes your final layer before the cheese layer.)

8. Place a double layer of *zoodles* on top.

9. Ladle $^1/_3$ portion of the red sauce on top, then another double layer of *zoodles*.

10. Repeat steps #7 to #9. Top off lasagna with the spinach-mushroom mix.

11. Sprinkle on the remaining cup of Romano cheese. Dot the surface with bits of mozzarella.

12. Place the dish inside the oven and bake for 45 to 60 minutes. Take out the dish immediately.

13. Let the lasagna cool for at least 15 minutes before slicing. Serve warm, at room temperature, or even chilled as leftovers next day.

**Cooking Tip:** when searing mushrooms in a skillet, fry only a few pieces at a time. Crowding the pan will only make the mushrooms release their juices faster. The mushrooms will cook unevenly and will not brown. If you have a large batch of mushrooms to cook, or if you have a small skillet, it is best to sear your mushrooms in batches.

## Recipe #20: Seafood Marinara with Rainbow Noodles

Serves 3 to 4

*Ingredients:*

### For the noodles

- ➤ 4 rashers, thick streaky bacon or *pancetta*, thinly sliced
- ➤ 1 piece, small carrot
- ➤ 1 piece, small sweet potato
- ➤ 1 piece, small zucchini
- ➤ ¼ piece, small summer squash
- ➤ salt, to taste
- ➤ black pepper, to taste
- ➤ ¼ cup water

### For the marinara sauce

- ➤ 1 pound mussels, shells scrubbed, beards removed
- ➤ 1 pound small clams, soaked in brine for at least an hour to remove the sand inside the shells, rinsed, drained (Create brine by dissolving ½ cup of regular salt in every 1 cup of water.)
- ➤ 1 pound shrimps, shelled, deveined
- ➤ 1 Tbsp. olive oil
- ➤ 1 can crushed tomatoes, lightly drained
- ➤ 1 cup fish or vegetable stock

- ➤ 4 cloves, large garlic, minced
- ➤ 2 pieces, large tomatoes, deseeded, minced
- ➤ 1 piece, large shallot, minced
- ➤ 1 piece, large fresh jalapeno chili, minced
- ➤ 1 Tbsp. tomato paste
- ➤ 2 tsp. lemon juice, freshly squeezed
- ➤ 1 tsp. Spanish or sweet paprika
- ➤ 1 tsp. oregano powder
- ➤ 1 tsp. thyme powder
- ➤ 1 piece, small lemon, sliced into wedges, for garnish

*Directions:*

1. <u>To make the noodles</u>: place the bacon and water in a skillet set over high heat. Let the water come to a full boil, then wait for most of the liquid has evaporated, about 10 minutes.

2. When the skillet is relatively dry, turn down to medium heat. Let the fat render out of the bacon, and wait for the latter to crisp up. This should take another 10 minutes.

3. Remove the skillet off the heat. Scoop out the bacon bits and transfer to a plate where these can cool completely. Reserve the bacon grease for the vegetables.

4. Preheat the oven to 400°F or 205°C. Line a baking sheet with parchment paper.

5. Using **Blade B**, turn your carrots, sweet potatoes, summer squash, and zucchini into thick noodles, cutting off at 6-inch long strands. Set aside in a large mixing bowl.

6. Pour a few tablespoons of the bacon grease on the *zoodles*. Season lightly with salt and pepper. Toss gently.

7. Transfer the prepared *zoodles* on to the baking dish. Try to space out the noodles to ensure even cooking.

8. Bake the vegetables in the oven for 20 minutes, but toss lightly midway through the cooking process.

9. Take the baking sheet out of the oven immediately, and let the *zoodles* cool for a few minutes on the kitchen counter before using.

10. To make the marinara: place the olive oil in a large saucepan set over medium heat.

11. Stir fry the shallot and garlic together, until the former turns limp and transparent.

12. Stir in the fresh and canned tomatoes.

13. Pour in the rest of the marinara ingredients, except for the bacon bits, clams, mussels, shrimps, and the lemon wedges. Turn up the heat to the highest setting. Partially place the lid on the saucepan, and let the sauce come to a boil.

14. Add in the clams, mussels and shrimp. Place the lid on tightly, count slowly from 1 to 10, then turn off the flame. The residual heat will cook the seafood through.

15. Check on your shellfish after 10 minutes.

16. Scoop out the clams, mussels and shrimp and transfer these to a small bowl.

17. Place the saucepan over medium heat again, and cook until the sauce is reduced by half.

18. To assemble: put one portion of the cooked *zoodles* on a plate. Place a few pieces of clams, mussels and shrimp on top. Ladle about ½ cup of marinara sauce after. Garnish with bacon bits.

Serve the dish immediately with a wedge of lemon on the side. Spritz the dish with lemon sauce just before eating.

# Chapter 6: Beverages

### Recipe #21: Apples and Pears in Honey Lemon Juice

Serves 3 to 4

*Ingredients:*

- ➤ 1 piece, small pear
- ➤ 1 piece, small apple
- ➤ 1 piece, large lemon
- ➤ 1 Tbsp. honey
- ➤ 1 liter filtered water

You will also need:

- ➤ A large pitcher or large non-reactive container that will fit into your fridge.

*Directions:*

1. Dissolve honey in the filtered water. Stir well.
2. Using **Blade A**, slice the pear and apple into thin disks. Drop the disks into the filtered water.
3. Using a food grater, zest the lemon, then squeeze out the juice. Pour these into the filtered water.
4. Chill the juice for at least an hour. Strain before serving. Always serve cold.

**Cooking tip:** cucumbers can become too watery. After slicing, place these on paper towels or strain these in the colander to remove excess moisture... unless you are adding these in drinks!

## Recipe #22: Cucumber and Pear Infusion

Serves 3 to 4

*Ingredients:*

➤ 3 pieces, large cucumbers

➤ 1 piece, small pear

➤ 1 piece, large lemon

➤ 1 liter filtered water

You will also need:

➤ A large pitcher or large non-reactive container that will fit into your fridge.

➤ A muddler, or a wooden spoon

*Directions:*

1. Using **Blade A**, slice the cucumbers and pears. Drop these into the filtered water.

2. Using a vegetable peeler, zest the lemon, then squeeze out the juice. Pour these into the filtered water.

3. Using a muddler, bruise the cucumber and pear to release more flavor.

4. Chill the infusion for at least an hour.

5. Strain before serving. Always serve cold.

**Juicing tip:** the best pear varieties to use in the spiralizer are: Anjous, Asian, *Comice*, French butter pears and Seckel. Avoid using: Bartletts, and Bosc which are too soft and will often crumble under the blade.

## Recipe #23: Chunky Carrot and Orange Juice

Serves 3 to 4

*Ingredients:*

➢ 2 pieces, large carrots

➢ 4 pieces, large juicing oranges

➢ ¾ liter filtered water

➢ ½ cup white sugar, add more if desired

You will also need:

➢ A large pitcher or large non-reactive container that will fit into your fridge.

*Directions:*

1. Dissolve sugar into filtered water. Stir well.

2. Using **Blade C**, slice the carrots into long, thin noodles. Chop these into finer pieces using a sharp knife. Drop the carrots into the water. (You can also lightly pulse the carrots in a food processor.)

3. Peel the oranges, and divide into segments. Drop segments into the water. Squeeze the core of the oranges to extract as much juice as possible. Pour juice into the water too.

4. Chill the drink for at least an hour before serving. Always serve cold.

**Juicing Tip:** the best juicing orange varieties are *navels* and *Valencia*, but you can always use blood oranges for a more striking color. You can substitute other citruses, like: *calamondin,* grapefruits, lemons, and limes. Just remember to take out the pips.

## Recipe #24: Spiked Cucumber-Pineapple Tea with Rum and Mint (for Adults only!)

Serves 7

*Ingredients:*

- ➤ 4 bags black tea
- ➤ 4 cups water, for chilling
- ➤ 3 cups water, for boiling
- ➤ 1 cup spiced dark rum or bourbon
- ➤ 1 cup fresh pineapple chunks
- ➤ 1 cup, loosely packed fresh mint leaves
- ➤ ½ cup pineapple concentrate (organic)
- ➤ ½ cup white sugar
- ➤ 1 piece cucumber, chilled
- ➤ pineapple wedges, for garnish, optional

You will also need:

- ➤ 3-quart pitcher or large non-reactive container that will fit into your fridge
- ➤ 2-quart saucepan
- ➤ Fine mesh strainer

*Directions:*

1. In a 2-quart saucepan, bring 3 cups of water to a boil. Turn off the heat. Pour in the 4 bags of tea and the fresh mint. Let the tea steep for 10 minutes with the lid on.

2. Strain out the tea bags and mint leaves. Discard.

3. Dissolve sugar in the warm water.

4. Combine tea-infused water, with the cold water and pineapple concentrate. Chill for at least 1 hour before serving.

5. Using **Blade A**, slice the cucumber into long, flat noodles. Chop noodles into 4-inch long strands. Drop the cucumber in the tea just before serving.

6. Mix in the rum.

7. Pour tea into tall glasses and garnish with pineapple wedges, if using.

# Recipe #25: Jicama and Red Beets Infusion

Serves 3 to 4

*Ingredients:*

- ➢ 1 piece, large jicama, peeled, quartered
- ➢ 1 piece, large apple
- ➢ 2 pieces, large red or sugar beets, peeled
- ➢ 1 liter filtered water
- ➢ ¼ cup apple juice concentrate
- ➢ ¼ cup honey

<u>You will also need:</u>

- ➢ A large pitcher or large non-reactive container that will fit into your fridge

*Directions:*

1. Using **Blade A**, slice the apple, beets and jicama into thin disks.
2. Drop the fruits into the filtered water.
3. Stir in the apple juice concentrate and honey.
4. Chill for at least an hour before serving. Always serve cold.

**Cooking tip:** to make it easier to fit oddly shaped fruits and vegetables within the brackets of the spiralizer, chop off the ends evenly using a sharp knife. Then, with a vegetable peeler, shave off more problematic areas (e.g. corners or indentations.)

# Chapter 7: Tips on How to Make the Most Out of Your Spiralizer

Like all machines worth investing in, you need to take better care of your spiralizer. This will extend its lifespan, and provide you more years of service. So here are a few easy tips you can try.

➢ Buy a separate brush for your machine. Most spiralizers are dishwasher-safe, but it would still be better if you can scrub the blades using a dedicated brush. Sometimes, fruit or vegetable fibers remain within the blades. These leftovers will contribute to the early decay of the metal, and leave offensive odors. Buy a small scrubbing brush that you will use only for your spiralizer.

➢ Always wash the blades with soapy water to prevent scratches.

➢ Always air dry or pat dry the machine and its separate components before storing these away to prevent the metal from decaying. This prevents mold from finding roots in the nooks and crannies of your spiralizer.

➢ Use your spiralizer for fruits and vegetables only. Use the cheese grater for grating cheese. Use the apple corer for removing apple cores. Use the cherry pitter to remove cherry pits. You get the idea.

➢ Use your spiralizers for hardier fruits and vegetables only. If fruits and vegetables are too soft, these will only turn into mush when your process these. You might want to try using other cutting/slicing implements for delicate food items.

# Conclusion

I hope this book was able to provide you more ideas on how to make the most out of your spiralizer. There are many great fruits and vegetables that you can turn into healthy *zoodles*. If you are on any kind of diet, adding more fruits and vegetables to your daily meals is always a great thing. Best of all, you can sneak fresh greens in everything: from breakfast items, to pasta dishes, and even in your drinks.

The next step is to recreate your favorite meals using your spiralizer. Better yet, there might be recipes in this book that you can turn into your *new* favorites. You can share these dishes with friends and family who will love the fun shapes in your soups, stews and beverages.

If you find this book informative, please take the time to give it a 5 star rating.

I wish you the best of luck!

*John Web*

Made in the USA
Middletown, DE
14 November 2016